Maximizing Opportunities

Networking with Advanced Communication Skills

Table of Contents

Chapter 1. Introduction

In an interconnected world, where opportunities can often present themselves from the most unexpected of sources, mastering the art of networking and showcasing your advanced communication skills becomes vitally pivotal. But how does one accurately navigate this dynamic and fast-paced landscape? This is where our Special Report "Maximizing Opportunities: Networking with Advanced Communication Skills" comes into play. This insightful report aims to guide you on your journey towards achieving breakthroughs, by leveraging the power of effective networking and superior communication. Think of it as your roadmap, leading you towards a radiant horizon of endless potential. Enriched with practical tips, expert advice, and compelling narratives, this report is sure to inspire, motivate and equip you with the tools to unlock doors you never even knew existed. So, embark on this exciting voyage, discover your untapped potential, and let's revolutionize the way you network!

Chapter 2. Mastering the Basics: Principles of Effective Networking

Understanding the nuances and significance of networking can emerge as a daunting task for many. Yet, it remains an irrefutable truth that robust networking skills can act as a stepping stone towards unimagined potential and opportunities. This chapter aims to demystify the realm of networking and bring to light the principle attributes that constitute effective networking.

2.1. Establishing the Right Mindset

The outset of any journey in the realm of networking composes of adopting the accurate mindset. This is a crucial factor as your outlook towards networking can dramatically underpin its effectiveness. You should not see networking as a mere means to an end but rather as a journey of forming meaningful connections. It's about building relationships that can provide mutual benefits. By keeping this as the bedrock of your networking strategy, you transform the entire experience to a rewarding process of personal and professional growth.

2.2. Building your Networking Strategy

A networking strategy consists of identifying your goals, targeting the correct audience, choosing the right platforms and consistently nurturing these relationships. Also, try to incorporate parameters such as networking frequency, methods (both online and offline) and a continuity plan in case of unforeseen circumstances. Regularly review and adapt your strategy to meet the ever-changing networking landscape.

2.3. Choosing the Right Platforms

Your choice of networking platforms can significantly impact the effectiveness of your networking efforts. Realize that nowadays there are multifarious virtual platforms in addition to traditional in-person meetings and events. Ensure to choose platforms that align with your target audience. For example, a platform like LinkedIn can be more useful if you want to network with professionals and business owners.

2.4. Effective Communication Techniques

Undeniably, an essential aspect of networking is communication. Mere self-expression will not be effective unless coupled with active listening, empathy, and emotional intelligence. Acquainting yourself with these skills and integrating them into your networking approaches can significantly enhance your networking experiences.

2.5. Nurturing and Maintaining Connections

Building connections is a singular part of your networking journey; nurturing them is what makes networking an ongoing process. Regularly touch base with your contacts and show genuine interest in their activities. Even if you don't need any immediate assistance or favor, keeping the connection alive goes a long way in maintaining fruitful relationships.

2.6. Understanding the Power of Reciprocity

Reciprocity stands as a golden rule in networking. If someone assists you, ensure that you return the favor whenever possible. This will not only deepen your relationship but also incentivize them to help you further, thereby creating a mutually beneficial association.

2.7. Representing yourself Appropriately

People prefer to network with those who show genuine interest, respect, and positive attitude. Keeping a professional demeanor, positive attitude, and being respectful of others' time and presence can uplift your perception among your network.

2.8. Tackling Obstacles

Just as any other endeavor, networking too is likely to come with its share of uncertainties and hurdles. However, it is essential to acknowledge them and learn from these experiences. Your errors act as stepping stones for improvement.

2.9. Concluding Thoughts

Effective networking is an extensive, ongoing process that requires consistent effort, aptitude, and a positive approach. Master these core principles and adapt them to your networking strategy. And remember, the horizon is reachable if you dare to voyage. This is your journey, a journey enriched with opportunities, lessons, and immense growth potential.

In the forthcoming sections, we'll fixate on advanced communication skills and how to amalgamate them into your networking tactics, leading to enriched and deeper connections, guiding you towards unimagined opportunities.

Chapter 3. Body Language: Unspoken Communication in Networking

A vital component of effective communication often underestimated is body language. The subtle nuances of non-verbal cues can make or break a networking opportunity. Ignorance or misinterpretation of these cues can lead to unnecessary confusion or misrepresentation.

3.1. Beginning with the Basics

Understanding body language begins with awareness of your own body. Recognizing or acknowledging the way your body acts and reacts in various situations is the first step towards mastering non-verbal communication. Invest time in observing your natural gestures, expressions, postures, and body movements. Use a mirror or videotape yourself during a mock conversation to gain insight. Once you become aware of your body, gradually start regulating your movements so that they translate into a powerful, effective non-verbal language during interactions.

3.2. The Importance of Eye Contact

While engaging in conversation, maintaining good eye contact plays a key role. It demonstrates your interest and attentiveness towards the person and the conversation. Breaking eye-contact too frequently or avoiding it altogether could convey disinterest or dishonesty. However, don't mistake staring for maintaining eye contact. It's recommended that you hold eye contact for roughly 60% of the conversation to appear invested but not aggressive.

3.3. Positioning: A Reflection of Attitude

The positioning of your body has a significant impact on how people perceive your disposition. Open body language – standing tall with shoulders back, not crossing your arms or legs – makes you seem approachable and interested. In comparison, closed body language – folding your arms across your chest or hunching over – sends out signals of disinterest, defensiveness, or insecurity.

3.4. Gestures: Amplifying the Message

Gestures, when used correctly, add power and enthusiasm to your communication. Simple gestures like nodding can show that you're listening and interested. However, overusing or under-using gestures can interrupt the flow of communication. Aim for a balance.

3.5. Mirroring: A Silent Compliment

People tend to like those who are similar to themselves. In the realm of body language, mirroring the positive body language of the person you are speaking to can lead to positive rapport. However, it should be subtly implemented to avoid the appearance of mockery.

3.6. Facial Expressions: A Window to Emotions

Understanding and correctly interpreting facial expressions can provide a wealth of information about the person's emotional state. Similarly, keeping control and being aware of your facial expressions can highly influence the impression you create.

3.7. The Power of Personal Space

Understanding the concept of personal space in networking helps in creating comfort during interaction. Invading someone's personal space – standing or sitting too close – can create discomfort and may often be perceived as dominance or aggression. Respect the personal space and judge the comfort level through the individual's body language cues.

3.8. Touch: A Tricky Territory

Using touch in professional settings can be tricky. While a firm handshake reflects confidence, undue or unasked physical contact can be seen as a violation of respect and space.

3.9. Interpreting Mixed Signals

Often, body language signals are mixed, leading to confusion in understanding the message being communicated. Careful observation over time, understanding the individual's communication style, context, and corroborating it with verbal communication can help decipher mixed signals accurately.

3.10. The Final Word: Consistency

Consistency between verbal and non-verbal communication is crucial. Incongruencies can lead to doubts about the authenticity of the message or the narrator.

Navigating the sea of networking can be challenging, but understanding body language and harnessing its power can act as a lighthouse, guiding you away from potential obstacles and towards successful interactions. As with any skill, continuous practice and conscious effort turns these learned behaviours into instinctive responses, enhancing your communication further.

Remember, "The most important thing in communication is hearing what isn't being said." - Peter Drucker. Body language is that unspoken communication. Master it, and you unlock a myriad of opportunities in the networking domain.

Chapter 4. The Art of Listening: Valuable Insights from Silent Conversations

In our high-speed, multi-tasking world, listening is a lost art. Yet, it is a crucial skill for successful networking and communication. One can only harness the power of silence if they can truly understand the value of active listening. A silent conversation, often overpowered by the noise of our preconceived notions, egos and impatience, needs to be tuned purposefully; it is during this silence, when words are absent, can one decode the most profound understandings and insights.

4.1. The Science Behind Listening

Listening is not merely the passive act of receiving sound waves through the ear. Rather, it is a complex process involving several stages—receiving, decoding, understanding, remembering, evaluating, and responding. Each stage has a purpose, each tuned to unravel another layer of the spoken words, to understand the thoughts that remain unexpressed.

We listen to gather information, to learn and understand, to show empathy, and to build relationships. While we often equate verbal eloquence as a measure of effective communication skills, it's our ability to listen that sets successful communicators apart. Our silence can often prompt the speaker to reveal more; our attentive posture can encourage them to dig deeper into their thoughts, and our responsive and timely nods can assure them of our involvement.

It's important to remember the words of 'Epictetus', the Greek philosopher, who said, "We have two ears and one mouth so that we can listen twice as much as we speak".

4.2. The Power of Active Listening

Active listening requires more than just hearing the words that are spoken. It implies absorbing the complete message being delivered verbally and non-verbally. Active listeners are engaged listeners. They resist all distractions, provide feedback, ask relevant questions, and reflect on what has been heard.

How often have you found that despite being 'heard', you didn't feel 'listened to'? This often occurs when the listener is tuned off, mentally preoccupied, or simply indifferent. Conversely, when someone listens to you actively, you feel valued, cared for, and important.

Imagine how much a simple act of active listening can boost your networking abilities! People would not just acknowledge you as a great communicator, but also perceive you as an empathetic and caring individual they can trust and connect with.

4.3. Practical Strategies to Enhance Listening Skills

How can you become an active listener? Here are some strategies.

1. Subdue Internal Noise: Often, our mind races with countless thoughts which distract us and prevent genuine listening. Practice mindfulness. Clear your mind and focus on the speaker completely.

2. Practice Empathy: Put yourself in the other person's shoes. Understand their perspective and feelings.

3. Note Non-Verbal Cues: The unspoken can sometimes speak volumes. Observe the speaker's body language, the fluctuations in their tone, the fluctuation in their emotions.

4. Ask Clarifying Questions: Questions reflect your interest and want to understand better.

5. Provide Feedback: It reassures the speaker and indicates your engagement in the conversation.

4.4. From Listening to Responding: The Art of Constructive Feedback

How you respond to a speaker's thoughts can either encourage communication or completely shut it down. Constructive feedback demonstrates active listening and fosters positive relationships.

Follow the 'Praise-Improve-Praise' pattern while providing feedback. Start and end with a positive note. Sandwich your suggestions for improvement in between. This leaves the speaker feeling valued and more open to constructive feedback.

4.5. In Conclusive Thoughts

Embedding these practices into your communication can indeed be challenging. However, the rewards far outweigh the efforts. The art of listening silently cultivates genuine empathy, fosters deeper connections, and opens up a world of hidden insights. It's the crux of successful networking.

As you journey through the wide and vibrant landscape of networking, remember to pause, listen, and indulge in meaningful conversations. Start observing, understanding, and valuing the silent conversations around you. The insights harvested would not only guide your decisions but will also make you a more intuitive, reflexive, and skilled communicator. Remember, the most profound insights can sometimes echo in the silence.

Chapter 5. Online Networking: Making Virtual Connections Count

A foray into online networking may seem daunting initially—but fear not. Technology implores us to seize the potential of this digital sphere, where infinite connections and possibilities reside. The key, however, lies in understanding how to leverage these online avenues effectively.

5.1. Understanding the Digital Landscape

To reap the benefits of online networking, we need to first appreciate the platform diversity that the digital landscape boasts. Websites, social media platforms, blogs, forums, e-commerce sites—each of these are ripe with networking opportunities, albeit varying in their methods, formality, and etiquette. A well-rounded networking approach encompasses them all.

Online networking strategies differ immensely based on the platform at hand. LinkedIn, for instance, necessitates a professional and concise approach. Twitter, on the other hand, prizes brevity and wit. Instagram encourages visual communication, while Facebook and other forums value personal storytelling and long-form content.

5.2. Building a Robust Online Presence

The cornerstone of a phenomenal networking strategy begins with creating a strong online identity. This encompasses your personal brand and signals your attributes, skills and experiences to others. Here are some tips to help steer you in the right direction:

1. Always keep your profile information up-to-date.

2. Opt for high-quality profile and cover photos that reflect your personal brand.

3. Develop a compelling "About" section or bio that provides a snapshot of who you are.

4. Showcase your expertise and experience.

5. Recommend others and seek recommendations – building reciprocal relationships amplifies your trustworthiness.

6. Share quality content regularly to confirm your activity and formidable knowledge on relevant subjects.

5.3. Practicing Proactive Outreach

Online networking is not a spectator sport. Participate in discussions, provide thoughtful comments, and engage positively with content in your field. This expands your visibility, demonstrating your interest and expertise concurrently. Focus on relationship-building for sustainable networking rather than quick transactions. Send personalized and context-specific connection requests to avoid coming across as spammy or insincere.

5.4. Navigating Virtual Networking Events

Virtual events such as webinars, online conferences, and meetups present unique networking opportunities. RSVP promptly and attend diligently. Make use of chat functions during live events for thoughtful interaction and follow-up with attendees post-event through social platforms or emails. This proactive approach establishes your commitment to these professional relationships.

5.5. Leveraging the Power of Content

Contributing original content is another avenue to authenticate your expertise, instigate discussions, and garner visibility. Blog posts, podcasts, webinars, white papers, infographics, or social media posts—attractive and informative content has the inherent power to multiply your outreach.

5.6. Mastering the Follow-Up

Timely and personalized follow-ups are the linchpin for nurturing online relationships. Such interactions could reaffirm the insights shared or discussions had, thus providing a thoughtful touchpoint that strengthens this newfound connection.

5.7. Ensuring Privacy and Security Online

Practice discretion in sharing personal information. Never forget to apply strict privacy settings — curated for each platform — to ensure your security online.

In conclusion, the possibilities of online networking are as vast as the digital landscape itself. By fostering strategic actions—building a robust online presence, practicing proactive outreach, navigating virtual networking events, leveraging the power of content, mastering the art of follow-ups, and ensuring privacy—this intricate web of virtual connections can indeed be demystified. With commitment, the often-overwhelming world of online networking can transform relationships into opportunities, marking the dawn of limitless professional horizons.

Chapter 6. Cross-Cultural Communication: Harnessing Diversity in your Network

In a globalized world, your networking efforts will inevitably lead you across cultural boundaries. Understanding cross-cultural communication and incorporating its principles into your networking can transform and expand your professional relationships.

6.1. Understanding Different Cultures

Understanding different cultures begins with acknowledging that our own cultural context heavily influences the way we communicate. Recognizing the variability in communication styles across cultures allows us to nurture richer, deeper connections.

Broadly, different cultures can exhibit attitudes ranging from individualistic to collectivistic, measured on a scale known as the Hofstede's Cultural Dimensions Theory. Individualistic cultures, like those in the United States, prioritize personal achievement and independence over group harmony. In contrast, collectivist cultures, like those in Japan and many other Asian countries, value group harmony and societal norms over personal achievement. This fundamental difference can manifest in contrasting communication strategies and behavior in professional settings.

In the context of networking, understanding such differences can help you approach interactions with sensitivity, empathy, and respect. This foundational knowledge enables us to shape our communication based on the cultural background and preferences of our counterparts.

6.2. Non-verbal Communication Across Cultures

Non-verbal communication includes facial expressions, body language, eye contact, spatial arrangements, and even silence. It often conveys more information than verbal communication and can differ drastically across cultures.

For instance, maintaining eye contact is viewed as a sign of honesty and trustworthiness in many Western cultures. Conversely, in some Asian cultures, less direct eye contact may represent respect towards elders or superiors. The use of silence can also differ; while often seen as awkward or uncomfortable in Anglo-Saxon cultures, silence is highly respected and can signify deep thought or respect in Asian cultures.

Embracing an understanding of these non-verbal communication norms can help prevent misunderstandings when networking with individuals from diverse backgrounds, enabling smoother and more fruitful exchanges.

6.3. Bridging Communication Gaps: Tips and Strategies

Let's delve into practical ways you can bridge these communication gaps and maximize the potential of your diverse network.

1. Do Your Homework: Before interacting with someone from a different culture, research about their cultural norms, communication style, and etiquette. This preparation will help you approach the conversation with cultural sensitivity.

2. Practice Active Listening: Display genuine interest in what the other person is saying. Seek to clarify any confusion promptly to ensure mutual understanding.

3. Respect Differences: Treat each person as an individual and avoid stereotype-based assumptions. Show appreciation for diverse perspectives and be willing to adapt your communication strategies.

4. Seek Feedback: Regularly solicit feedback to ensure your messages are being correctly understood, and be open to adjusting your approach as necessary.

5. Build Trust: Trust forms the foundation of any networking relationship. Be reliable, keep your promises, and treat others with respect to build long-lasting relationships.

6.4. Leveraging Cultural Diversity

Embracing cultural diversity can enrich your networking experience and foster innovation. A wide range of perspectives can ignite creativity, increase problem-solving capacity, and provide distinct insights into international markets.

Incorporating a global mindset into your networking endeavors can not only build deeper connections but also unlock new opportunities in the global arena. It's key to harness the opportunities that diversity brings, and use it as a powerful catalyst for personal and professional growth.

6.5. Case Study: Cross-Cultural Communication in Action

Let's take an example of how effective cross-cultural communication can benefit networking. In a global tech company, they regularly facilitated cross-cultural forums where employees from various countries and teams could interact and learn about each other's cultures. This open dialogue encouraged appreciation for diversity and improved communication among geographically dispersed teams. As a result, employees built stronger networks globally, leading to higher collaboration and innovative breakthroughs in various projects.

6.6. Overcoming Challenges and Building Bridges

Remember, each interaction is a learning experience and it's okay to make mistakes. Adopt a lifelong learner mindset and view every misstep as a learning opportunity rather than a setback.

Harnessing diversity in your networking journey, while challenging, will open vast avenues of opportunities. Through your increased ability to network with individuals and groups from various cultures, you can access a broader, more diverse array of opportunities that might have been previously invisible.

With the increasingly interconnected world that we live in, the ability to effectively engage in cross-cultural communication has never been more valuable. As this skill is honed and refined, so too will your capacity to form beneficial professional relationships in your networking endeavors. Embrace the joy of learning about new cultures, the excitement of shared understanding, and the growth that can come from successfully navigating the challenges and rewards of cross-cultural communication in networking.

Chapter 7. Building Rapport: Creating an Endearing Presence

"A journey of a thousand miles begins with a simple hello." To achieve a meaningful journey in your networking voyage, it is paramount to recognize, understand and master the art of building rapport. Mastering rapport is more than just being friendly, it is about making an intimate connection that goes above and beyond a casual interaction.

7.1. Understanding Rapport: Beyond Just 'Getting Along'

Rapport is an understanding, a harmony that two or more individuals share when they are 'on the same wavelength'. It is not established by mere small talk. It focuses on exploring areas of common ground but goes beyond to create an affinity that is both authentic and endearing.

Rapport is a potent tool as it forms the basis of trust, without which you may struggle to efficiently network. It paves the way for meaningful conversations and effective communication that forms the core of prosperous networking realms.

7.2. The Science of Building Rapport: Adaptation and Mirroring

Building rapport might feel like an art, but rest assured – the science behind building early rapport is extensively studied and explained. The process involves two significant steps: adaptation and mirroring.

Adaptation, in this context, requires adjusting to the other person's communication style. This involves modeling their language, both verbal and non-verbal, and the pace, pitch, and tonality of their voice. It allows the person you are interacting with to feel 'in sync' with you.

Mirroring is a psychological strategy that involves subtly copying the body language, behaviors, or vocal cues of the person you are engaging with. By subtly mimicking these elements, one can create a sense of harmony and familiarity.

Remember, the key here is subtlety. Overt mirroring might come across as mockery. Practice this skill until it feels natural and effortless. It's not about imitating but creating a mirrored reflection.

7.3. Genuine Interest: The Heart of Rapport

A profound way to build rapport is to take a genuine interest in those with whom you are networking. Ask about their experiences, interests, ambitions, and challenges. Dale Carnegie, author of 'How to Win Friends and Influence People,' once said, "To be interesting, be interested."

Equally essential is the act of actively listening. While the person shares, ensure your responses are engaged and reflective of understanding. Active listening involves more than just quiet pauses; it's about validation, empathy, summary, and reciprocation.

The more you listen and display genuine interest, the more the person feels valued, heard, and thus more inclined to open up to you.

7.4. Tapping Into Empathy: Connection Through Understanding

Empathy forms the stepping stone towards genuine rapport. Strive to understand your counterparts' thoughts, feelings, and perspectives – delve into their shoes and capture their world through their lens. Try to grasp their emotional state, and most importantly, communicate that understanding to them.

This doesn't mean agreeing with every stance they hold but acknowledging and validating their feelings or thoughts without judgement. It creates a safe space inspiring trust, inviting deeper conversation, and promoting connectedness.

7.5. Storytelling: A Powerful Tool for Rapport Building.

The power of storytelling is often underestimated. It's not merely a form of entertainment; it's a tool for reaching out, resonating, and establishing an emotional connection.

Narrating personal experiences allows for vulnerability, which is a vital element in rapport building. It presents you as an open book, initiating a bond on a more personal level. Simultaneously, it provides a platform for them to relate, share, and feel more comfortable with you.

Stories also present the opportunity to share values, beliefs, and philosophy subtly. It helps the counterpart understand you better and see if there is aligning philosophy, creating yet another layer of connection.

Take note, however, that each interaction is a give-and-take. Avoid making every conversation about yourself.

7.6. Overcoming Barriers: Charting Through Difficult Waters

Building rapport does not always mean smooth sailing. Every person is unique, and you may face challenges aligning with some people you meet. Obstacles can include differences in culture, language, opinions, or even social awkwardness. Understanding, recognizing, and learning to navigate these barriers can significantly improve your rapport-building process.

Remember that rapport building is not an overnight achievement; instead, it's a nuanced process that requires patience and persistence. Consistent deposits of trust, empathy, keen interest, and understanding will eventually bear the fruits of a solid rapport.

7.7. Conclusion: Rapport, the Cornerstone of Successful Relationships

Rapport is the backbone of successful professional and personal relationships, armed with tools such as empathy and keen interest. Once you have it in your arsenal, you can quickly transform casual contacts into profound connections. A strong rapport can unlock doors to opportunities, influence, and success, making your networking journey a remarkable one. And remember, with each connection you forge, you deepen your understanding of the world and enrich your personal and professional life. Let's start transforming hellos into meaningful connections!

Chapter 8. Persistence and Consistency: The Underpinnings of a Robust Connection

To form a substantial, mutually beneficial connection, the undercurrents of persistence and consistency play an indispensable role. These twin pillars of networking come with their own subtleties, advantages, and challenges. Let's explore them in detail.

8.1. Understanding Persistence

Persistence is all about resolve and determination in the face of adversity. In the context of networking, persistence refers to the determination to stay engaged and maintain a consistent interaction, even when the connection might not seem profitable immediately. Persistence in networking, however, should not be confused with being intrusive. There is a fine line between intelligently persistent and aggressively desperate, and this is where the art of networking comes into play.

1. **The art of following up:** Following up is crucial in networking. Whether it's a casual network or a potential business connection, the follow-up demonstrates your sincere interest. However, you must be strategic and tactful when following up. Show interest and ask open-ended questions. A good follow-up message shows that you remember specific points from your conversation, thereby solidifying your interest and commitment.

2. **Understanding the balance:** Persistence requires finding the right balance between consistency and being overbearing. If you lean towards the latter, you risk alienating the person you wish to

network with. Therefore, decide prudently the frequency of your follow-ups and their contents.

8.2. Embracing Consistency

Unlike persistence, consistency is about the predictability of actions over a certain time period. In networking, you are perceived as reliable when you behave congruently in different contexts and over time.

1. **Value Proposition Consistency:** Your professional value proposition acts as a lighthouse, guiding others to understand you better. Ensure that this proposition remains consistent across all networking platforms. Be it LinkedIn, industry events, or even social gatherings - a consistent value proposition helps build credibility and recognition.

2. **Consistent Engagement:** Regular engagement forms the cornerstone of consistency in networking. Whether through sharing valuable insights, commenting on posts, or interacting within professional communities, consistent engagement strengthens the network bond.

8.3. Strategies for Persistence and Consistency

Let's now delve deeper into the strategies that can help you attain persistence and consistency in networking.

1. **Setting Follow-Up reminders:** In the plethora of interactions we indulge in today, it's easy to forget the follow-ups. Hence, developing a habit of setting follow-up reminders could be very helpful. There are multiple tools available, like networking apps, CRM software, or even the humble calendar reminders, that you can leverage.

2. **Establish Regular Communication:** Scheduled check-ins can be extremely effective in maintaining consistency. You can drop a text, email, or call every now and then, maintaining an equilibrium so that it does not turn into a forced communication.

3. **Content Strategy:** Regularly sharing industry insights, opinion pieces, or personal achievements keeps your network engaged and strengthens your professional image.

8.4. Overcoming Roadblocks and Challenges

Networking, persistence, and consistency – needless to point out, come with their unique challenges. Expect roadblocks, rejections, and unresponsive potential connections. Here, treat these challenges not as setbacks, but as opportunities to reflect, learn, and improve. Remember, every 'no' is a step closer to a 'yes'.

1. **Dealing with Rejection:** It's possible that your requests may be turned down or ignored. Instead of dwelling on the negativity, use this as an opportunity to understand and improve your approach. It is important to retain your confidence and continue your pursuit.

2. **Regular Evaluation:** Keep a check on the success rate of your networking efforts. It'll help assess what's working and what needs to change. Don't hesitate to alter your strategies periodically to align with your networking goals.

Remember, the core of networking lies not in taking, but in giving. Only when you are genuine, can persistence and consistency yield fruitful results. Your focus should always be on building relationships, offering value where you can, and waiting patiently for the moment when your efforts bear fruit.

Conclusion:

Successfully integrating persistence and consistency to your networking strategy may seem daunting initially; however, by approaching it tactically and genuinely, a robust network of valuable relationships can be built. Embrace the challenges that come along the way as stepping stones toward your networking mastery. With time, commitment, the right techniques, and a pinch of charisma, watch your networking game transform, unveiling possibilities beyond your wildest dreams.

Chapter 9. Overcoming Barriers: Dealing with Communication Missteps

Miscommunication is often at the root of much awkwardness and inefficiency, serving as a barrier to successful networking. From misunderstandings and inaccurate interpretations, to lack of clarity and articulation, several hiccups can prevent you from conveying your ideas and messages effectively. Recognizing and addressing these communication missteps, however, can substantially improve your networking efforts, turning misunderstandings into opportunities for learning and growth.

9.1. The Art of Active Listening

An essential component of communication is active listening. Unfortunately, many disregard its importance, creating a primary barrier to effective communication. Misinterpretations, overlooked details, and missed cues often stem from a failure to listen attentively.

To improve, try to focus entirely on the speaker and show active engagement in the conversation. Avoid multitasking or getting distracted by your thoughts. Reflect on what the speaker is saying and, if necessary, ask for clarification to avoid misunderstandings. Keep eye contact, provide affirmation signals, like nodding or saying 'uh-huh', and offer feedback when appropriate. This invests you more in the conversation and portrays you as a respectful listener.

9.2. Reading Body Language

The nuances of body language play a crucial role in interpersonal communication. Non-verbal cues can often convey more about a person's thoughts and feelings than their actual words. Therefore, a lack of ability to interpret these cues accurately can lead to communication missteps.

Consider practicing observing body language during conversations. Ensure to pay attention to facial expressions, eye contact, gestures, posture, and other non-verbal cues. Note that the context is paramount in interpreting these signals accurately, and if you feel unsure, ask directly. Over time, you'll hone your skills and become more adept at perceiving underlying messages.

9.3. Fostering Clarity and Conciseness

A principal challenge in communication is walking the fine line between providing enough information for understanding and preventing overwhelming your listener with excessive details. It is essential to deliver your point in a clear, concise, and accessible manner.

One way to achieve clarity and conciseness is to plan your communication beforehand. Identify your main points, organise your thoughts and craft your message to ensure it drives your point home effectively. If you tend to ramble, practice trimming down your speech by focusing more on your main ideas and less on side details.

9.4. Cultivating Emotional Intelligence

Strong emotional intelligence allows us to recognize, understand, and manage our own emotions, and indeed those of others. This skill is something of a master key in dealing with communication missteps.

When interacting with others, be aware of emotional undercurrents. If the mood seems to be shifting negatively, address it. Acknowledging one's feelings, whether your own or the other person's, can defuse tension and facilitate more authentic and productive dialogue.

9.5. Enhance Your Verbal and Written Skills

Improving verbal and written communication skills is crucial for avoiding communication missteps. Verbal skills can be improved by expanding your vocabulary, practicing public speaking, and becoming more mindful of your voice tone and speed. On the other hand, enhancing written skills involves focusing on grammar, punctuation, and clarity of content, as well as structuring your text logically.

9.6. Handling Difficult Conversations

Difficult conversations are an inevitable part of networking. It's important not to shy away from them but to handle them with grace and maturity. Being prepared, showing empathy, and maintaining a positive attitude can turn a challenging conversation into an opportunity for growth.

Remember, no one is born an excellent communicator. It is achieved through consistent effort, practice and by learning from missteps. Dedication to improving your skills can aid you in overcoming communication barriers and help you make the most of your networking opportunities.

These efforts may seem daunting initially, but remember that progress is incremental. As you continue to invest in improving your communication skills, you'll start to see the positive effects ripple through all aspects of your life. From improved relationships and broader networking opportunities to greater personal and professional success, the benefits are limitless. So, keep practicing, keep learning, and keep growing - the world of effective networking awaits you!

Chapter 10. Effective Networking Ethics: Maintaining Professionalism

In the realm of effective networking, maintaining a professional demeanor is the cornerstone upon which building fruitful relationships is predicated. It's an art which requires constant diligence and self-awareness, taking into account the various perspectives, backgrounds, and interests that each participant brings to the table. As such, understanding and embodying professional networking ethics is indispensable. These are not merely a set of rules but rather a code of conduct that embodies the respect, sincerity, and authenticity that become your guiding principles.

10.1. Respect for Diversity

The business universe is a colorful mosaic of individuals from diverse backgrounds, each with unique perspectives, experiences, and insights. It requires a refined sense of respect and consideration for this diversity to foster healthy professional relationships. A tenet of networking professional ethics is to recognize these differences openly and engage with them positively. It requires avoiding assumptions, stereotypes, or biases that may affect your interactions. Your networking engagements should constantly reflect a willingness to understand, accept, and respect these differences.

10.2. Confidentiality and Trust

In a professional setting, confidentiality is paramount. It builds trust, forms the backbone of long-lasting professional relationships, and fosters a comfortable environment for open conversations. Remember, any information shared within a networking relationship—whether about personal issues, business strategies, or insights—is meant to stay within that relationship unless explicitly stated otherwise. Breaching this trust might not just terminate a network connection, but also tarnish your reputation in the broader professional community.

10.3. Authentic Interest and Active Listening

Similar to personal relationships, effective professional relationships involve authentic interest in other parties. Display curiosity about others' work experiences, interests, and aspirations, while maintaining appropriate professionalism. It's equally as crucial to demonstrate active listening. This not only manifests as hearing what the other person is saying but also involves understanding it. Giving adequate responses, making suitable eye contact, and effectively reacting to the speaker's emotions shows you are present in the discussion, thereby fostering a healthier networking environment.

10.4. Professional Boundaries and Personal Spaces

Respecting personal space and professional boundaries forms another significant aspect of networking ethics. Aim to strike the perfect balance between being interested and being intrusive. While showing enthusiasm about others' professional lives, it's essential not to cross the line into personal spaces unless explicitly invited. Equally, it's crucial that boundaries are transparent regarding what you are comfortable with sharing.

10.5. Online Networking Ethics

In the current interconnected world, much of our networking

transpires online. Hence, it is incumbent upon us to maintain professionalism in this virtual space. Regular and prompt communication, appropriate tone and language, respect for digital privacy, prevention of unsolicited messages, are all facets of online networking ethics.

10.6. Representing Your Authentic Self

While networking is about presenting yourself to others, it's crucial not to misrepresent yourself or your capacities for immediate gain. Present your authentic self, discuss your genuine interests, and be honest about your capacity and skill set. This approach will foster long-term relationships built on trust.

10.7. Reciprocity and Mutuality

Building upon mutualism—where both parties contribute and derive benefits—is a core professional networking ethics. Whether it's sharing insights, providing support, or recommending opportunities, the principle of reciprocity is a foundational networking principle.

10.8. Honoring Commitments

Professional ethics involves honoring commitments made during networking. Whether it's a commitment to catch up over a cup of coffee, provide some information, or deliver on a corporate project, these commitments form the basis of trust and show that you are reliable.

In conclusion, professional networking is a long-term investment. It warrants patience, perseverance, and, importantly, a strong foundation of professional ethics. Incorporating these principles into your networking conduct is a sure way to foster vibrant, reliable, and fruitful professional relationships.

Chapter 11. Looking Ahead: The Future of Networking with AI and Digital Transformation

Artificial intelligence and digital transformation are rapidly altering the landscape of networking, with effects seeping into every niche and facet of business and personal communication. As with every technological shift, the key to leveraging these new opportunities is understanding the complexities, nuances, and potentials of this brave new world.

11.1. An Introduction to AI and Digital Transformation in Networking

AI refers broadly to machines programmed to mimic human behaviors, particularly learning and problem-solving. Over the past decade, we have witnessed AI evolve from simplistic algorithms to sophisticated cognitive systems capable of deep learning and artificial neural networks.

Parallelly, digital transformation, a buzzword in today's corporate parlance, implies utilizing digital technologies to modify or create new processes, culture, customer experiences, and value propositions. It acts as a catalyst encompassing everything from reimagining organizational structures to nurturing a cloud-driven ecosystem.

In the realm of networking, digital transformation could mean anything from virtual meetings to data analytics for strategic connectivity. Meanwhile, AI can personalize networking experiences, automate routine tasks, and go a step further by predicting connections that could be beneficial in the future.

11.2. The AI Effect: Personalizing Networking Experiences

AI has presented unprecedented scope for personalization in professional networking. Machine learning algorithms can analyze and understand patterns in past interactions, tailoring future networking experiences to align with personal goals, interests, and conversation styles.

Networking platforms utilize AI to recommend potential contacts by calibrating parameters such as common connections, shared interests, or geographical proximity. This precision-recommendation model ensures that networking efforts bear fruit—connecting people with synchronous value propositions.

Furthermore, with the advent of chatbots and virtual assistants, AI has started to augment the first steps of interaction. These digital beings can initiate conversations, handle general queries and even set up meetings, paving the way for more substantial discussion.

Advanced systems like IBM's Watson can conduct sentiment analysis, detect nuance in human conversation, and respond appropriately, adding another layer of personalization to automated interactions.

11.3. Digital Transformation: Reinventing the Networking Wheel

Digital transformation is causing a seismic shift in networking dynamics. Analysis of granular data has enabled strategic connective intelligence—allowing individuals and businesses to understand who they should connect with, when, and for what purpose. Smart platforms are connecting professionals based on data-derived insights rather than haphazard meeting hopping, thereby leading to fruitful networks being built.

Virtual gatherings, spurred by the global pandemic, have proved that valuable connections can be forged outside traditional networking domains. In the face of constraints, virtual platforms have transformed into hubs of networking, equipped with breakout rooms, networking lounges, and personalized meeting schedules. Users can build meaningful relationships, without the costs and constraints of travel.

Digital transformation is also reshaping the follow-up process. Professionals can now use platforms that integrate with their work calendars, email inboxes, chat spaces, and more, all while maintaining privacy rules. With reminders, personalized messages, and touchpoints, these tools ensure that connections are nurtured beyond the initial conversation.

11.4. AI & Digital Transformation: The Confluence

The intersection of AI and digital transformation is now the fulcrum of several promising networking breakthroughs. Intelligent applications are now using predictive analytics based on user behavior, networking habits, industry trends, and more, to suggest potential connections and even provide conversation starters.

On broader terms, AI-driven platforms have started suggesting events, webinars, and lectures based on the individual's past interests and future potential areas of growth. These platforms are transforming from reactive to proactive networking partners.

This convergence is also reducing entry barriers to networking. AI-driven translations and real-time captions are making it easier for people with differing abilities to participate. Meanwhile, virtual gatherings are opening doors for people who were previously excluded because of geographical constraints, time limitations, or budget restrictions.

11.5. In Conclusion: Embracing the AI-driven Digital Transformation

The future of networking undoubtedly lies in embracing AI and digital transformation. These technology changes allow us to redefine how we approach networking—making it more targeted, personalized, and efficient.

However, this transition is not without challenges. Privacy, data security, and fostering human connections in a digital world are essential issues that need to be adequately addressed. Trends in AI-enabled emotional recognition and digital empathy tools suggest plausible solutions, but ethical and procedural guidelines need to be clearly defined and rigorously followed.

As we stand at the precipice of this change, let's ensure we harness AI's potential and digital transformation effectively to create a networking paradigm that's robust, inclusive, considerate, and values-centric. The future is here, ready to be explored; let it not be an intimidating frontier, but a fascinating landscape filled with limitless opportunities.